To Jackie Ormes. I hope I did you justice.

And to Nancy Goldstein and the Ormes family,
thank you for your time and support.

Images on page 34 courtesy of the University of Michigan Press, from their title
Jackie Ormes: The First African American Woman Cartoonist, by Nancy Goldstein.

Visit us on the Web! rhcbooks.com

Educators and librarians, for a variety of teaching tools, visit us at RHTeachersLibrarians.com

Library of Congress Cataloging-in-Publication Data is available upon request.
ISBN 978-0-593-42654-8 (trade) | ISBN 978-0-593-42655-5 (lib. bdg.)
ISBN 978-0-593-42656-2 (ebook)

The artist used Photoshop, Clip Studio Paint, and Procreate to create the illustrations for this book.
The text of this book is set in 16-point Brandon Grotesque.
Interior design by Rachael Cole

MANUFACTURED IN CHINA
10 9 8 7 6 5 4 3 2 1
First Edition

Random House Children's Books supports the First Amendment and celebrates the right to read.

JACKIE ORMES
DRAWS THE
FUTURE

The REMARKABLE LIFE of a
PIONEERING CARTOONIST

by
LIZ MONTAGUE

RANDOM HOUSE STUDIO ▲ NEW YORK

Monongahela, Pennsylvania, had a quiet warmth, like fresh-baked cookies resting on a windowsill. The town stretched on for miles, over hills and through asphalt roads, right up to Zelda Jackson's front door.

Zelda was born a few miles up the road in Pittsburgh, on August 1, 1911, but it was in the rolling greenery of Monongahela that Zelda bloomed into childhood.

To Zelda, adventure hid from her the way the sun hides from the moon—always just out of reach.

Still, she sought it everywhere. Telling secrets with her older sister, Delores. Singing gospel songs in her AME Church choir. Carving bars of soap until her creations emerged as smooth as ivory.

Somewhere along the way, Zelda realized adventure didn't have to be caught—it could be created.

Entire worlds she'd never seen
before began to decorate every piece
of paper she could get her hands on.
A field she could run through as far
as her hand could draw. An ocean she
could color as blue as she liked.

Zelda's last name, Jackson, gave rise to her
nickname, Jackie. Jackie was still deciding who she
dreamed of becoming. As a student, she was generous
with her smiles and fearless with her pencil.

Jackie chronicled day-to-day life in the 1929 and 1930 Monongahela High School yearbooks. Each person who populated her little corner of the world became a character. Miniature drawings of classmates and teachers mingled on the pages to create life as she saw it.

Zelda Jackson

But Jackie wanted her world to expand. Even though she was still in high school, Jackie already deemed herself worthy of bigger things.

She decided to write to Mr. Robert L. Vann, publisher of the *Pittsburgh Courier*, a prominent Black newspaper, to inquire about a job. Jackie hoped her merit would travel through her letters like wind through an open window.

Thanks to her persistence, Jackie went from high school yearbook editor to *Pittsburgh Courier* freelance reporter. Because she was still a young girl with a watchful mother, the *Courier*'s sports editor escorted Jackie to her first assignment. Far from being queasy or intimidated by the boxing match she was tasked with writing about, Jackie loved it, leaning into the fast-paced grit of sports reporting.

Once graduation had come and gone, Jackie's natural next step was to move to Pittsburgh. Here, a proofreading job and a few freelance reporting gigs awaited her at the *Courier*. Jackie wrote about everything from police beats and court cases to human-interest stories. Pittsburgh was a city of smoke and steel, set permanently in gray scale. If Monongahela was a car starting, Pittsburgh was an engine revving, loud and bold.

Pittsburgh suited Jackie. The city kept pace with her,
walking in lockstep as she figured out just how big her
adventures could be and who she might share them with.

Before Earl Clark Ormes became Jackie's husband, he was a friend of a friend. He was a face in a crowd, a shy smile with kind eyes behind glasses. In 1931, their forty-five-year marriage had only just begun.

The highs and lows of life met them early on their journey, as they were still finding their footing in an ever-changing world.

Their daughter, named Jacqueline, passed away just before her fourth birthday.

As Jackie grieved, an idea came to her in the form of a character . . .

. . . Torchy Brown, a cheerful nightclub star who was quick-witted and always fashionable. Jackie immersed herself in the imaginary world of Torchy, chronicling her escapades as she traveled from the South to Harlem.

Torchy sold her farm animals for the train ticket to New York and took on life in the city with country-girl resilience.

Torchy gripped Jackie, mind and heart. So many people navigating segregation had made similar journeys from the South, and it was a story that needed to be told. Through Torchy, Jackie was sure she knew best how to tell it. The only people who needed convincing were her editors.

Of two things Jackie was certain: she could make people laugh, and she could draw. Somehow, mixing the two things allowed people to smile even when talking about painful subjects.

Over the years, Jackie's ability to be persistent had not diminished. Eventually, her editors had no choice but to give her a chance.

Torchy Brown in "Dixie to Harlem" found a home in the *Pittsburgh Courier* in 1937. It ran through the pages of the *Courier* for twelve months before Jackie took a seven-year break from professional drawing.

Those years were filled with moves across the Midwest during the tail end of the Great Depression. A new hope was brewing, and on that current of hope, Jackie and her husband were pulled to Chicago.

Chicago was an exhale, a new start to see what life had in store for them.

Jackie began taking classes at the Art Institute of Chicago. She'd never taken formal art classes; her raw talent had carried her this far.

But, shoulder to shoulder with classmates who all seemed to know more than she did, Jackie felt small. She could've run. She could've knocked over her easel and never come back. But she didn't. She kept returning and, gradually, her skills became sharper, her lines more refined.

One day, chin raised, shoulders squared, Jackie walked into the office of the *Chicago Defender* and asked for whoever was in charge. The clippings of her previous work, along with the confidence she seemed to radiate, spoke for themselves. Jackie was hired on the spot.

She started as an occasional writer and reporter, getting the lay of the land as she explored life at this new paper. But behind the scenes, day by day and sketch by sketch, new ideas began to take shape. Soon, Jackie was back at the drawing board.

These ideas came and went like leaves on the breeze. Some, like *Candy*, a short-lived comic published in the *Defender*, stuck—but most didn't.

It was hard to concentrate. World War II was coming to an end, but to Jackie, it seemed as if Black soldiers were leaving one war just to come home and face another. Racial equality felt a long way off. Too long.

Jackie wanted change.

As she looked around her South Side neighborhood, pencil in hand, she decided she was as good as anyone to speak up about the injustices in her community. Maybe with all she'd done, lived, and seen, she was uniquely suited to reach people her male colleagues couldn't.

With her stylish and impeccably drawn characters, Jackie knew she could make people look—but how could she make them listen?

The idea came like snow falling, a light dusting growing into a blizzard. The sketches seemed to fly from Jackie's hands, pages pouring from every thought.

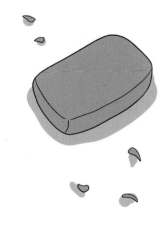

She'd found her protagonist: six-year-old Patty-Jo. Chaperoned by her older sister, Ginger, Patty-Jo spoke up about current events, wasn't shy about having an opinion, and wore a beautiful outfit every week.

She—and Jackie—would make the world listen.

MORE ABOUT JACKIE ORMES

Jackie Ormes, born Zelda Marvin Jackson (1911–1985), created bravely and fearlessly. Her four cartoon and comic series, which ran in Black newspapers intermittently from 1937 to 1956, depicted bold, dynamic women who inspired countless readers. Jackie's protagonists faced real-life issues with perseverance, confidence, and intelligence, directly combating the negative way Black female characters were often portrayed in the media.

One of her best-loved characters, Patty-Jo, lived within the single-panel cartoons of *Patty-Jo 'n' Ginger*, which would remain nestled between the pages of the *Pittsburgh Courier* for eleven years. Six-year-old Patty-Jo, chaperoned by her older sister, Ginger, offered a bitingly honest perspective on the day's news. Patty-Jo was as observant as she was fashionable, voicing many candid opinions that continue to be relevant.

With the cartoon's success—and noticing a gap in the market for Black dolls—Jackie harnessed her entrepreneurial skills to create a Patty-Jo doll. It would have Patty-Jo's signature look, along with an extensive wardrobe and play-friendly hair—a detail important to Jackie. She worked with the Terri Lee Doll Company to design a Patty-Jo doll, produced from 1947 to 1949, that became America's first upscale Black play doll. Patty-Jo is a collector's item today.

By creating a space for herself in the male-dominated world of cartooning, Jackie Ormes left an undeniable mark on the industry. Her contributions were posthumously honored when she was inducted into the National Association of Black Journalists Hall of Fame in 2014 and into the Will Eisner Comic Industry Hall of Fame in 2018.

Jackie Ormes

Pittsburgh Courier, August 9, 1947.
"All I ask for my birthday is a doll
that won't out-talk ME!"

Patty-Jo doll, circa 1947

AUTHOR'S NOTE

When I'm in tough situations or feeling hard things, I always tell myself: *Someone, somewhere, has done this before. Someone, somewhere, has felt this way.* It helps me feel less alone.

In 2019, I was fresh out of school, working a nine-to-five, and had just started contributing cartoons to the *New Yorker.* I was still very unsure of myself and my work, but I knew I wanted to say things I cared about. It's harder than you would think: to make characters who look like you when you look so different from most people in the space.

I kept asking myself, *How do I make work that feels true to me here?*

Even though I felt stuck and overwhelmed, I knew that someone, somewhere, looked like me and had done what I wanted to do.

One midnight Google wormhole later, I found Jackie Ormes. It was her boldness that stood out to me the most. To make work that honest and witty, in a time when most places still had a "Colored" section, left me stunned but smiling.

Jackie's work is as relevant and poignant now as it was over sixty years ago. Her bravery and creativity gave me a permission slip I didn't know I was looking for. I've been so honored to share Jackie's story, first for the *Nib* in 2019, then in 2020 for a Google Doodle, and now in this book you're holding.

More than once, I've created something and thought, *There's no way I can say this. It's too true, and I'm not brave enough to be this seen.* But as I hold my breath and submit it anyway, I remember: Jackie did it.

SELECTED SOURCES

Cavna, Michael. "The Rediscovered Legacy of Jackie Ormes, the First Black Woman with a Syndicated Comic Strip." *The Washington Post,* 19 Jan. 2018. washingtonpost.com/news/comic-riffs/wp/2018/01/19/the-rediscovered -legacy-of-jackie-ormes-the-first-black-woman-with-a-syndicated-comic-strip

"Comics Crusader: Remembering Jackie Ormes." *All Things Considered,* NPR, 29 July 2008. npr.org/2008/07/29/93029000/comics-crusader-remembering-jackie-ormes

"Facing the Music." Library of Congress. loc.gov/exhibitions/drawn-to-purpose/about-this-exhibition/early-comics /facing-the-music

Goldstein, Nancy. *Jackie Ormes: The First African American Woman Cartoonist.* University of Michigan Press, 2008.

Sayej, Nadja. "The Subtle Radicalism of Cartoonist Jackie Ormes." Shondaland, 6 March 2019. shondaland.com/live /a26668329/jackie-ormes-comic-radicalism

skleefeld. "1953 Jackie Ormes Profile." YouTube, 1 Feb. 2011. youtube.com/watch?v=gmdHOkB1SHA